To order additional copies of this book, contact us on Instagram *@myeverydayheroesmyinspiration*

2nd Edition

ISBN Hardback 978-981-14-8929-7
ISBN Paperback 978-981-14-8928-0
ISBN E-book 978-981-14-8930-3

Printed by
MYPRINT SHOP
Taman Maluri, Cheras,
55100KL, MALAYSIA

MY EVERYDAY HEROES,

MY INSPIRATION!

Bhavina Farswani

gratitude

To my Mom & Dad... thank you for always encouraging and supporting me. I will love you forever!

A big salute to all those who have been our frontline heroes before and during this pandemic. They work tirelessly to create a safe haven for everyone. Thank you!

~ Bhavina

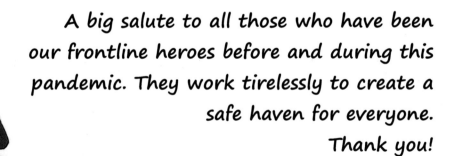

Thank you, My teachers!

"I am impressed by your interest in writing this book about such a diverse group of heroes. Your inquiry teaches the reader a lot about each person's purpose, interests and contributions to the world."
Kent Peterson, International School Teacher

"I am so proud of the success Bhavina is having and what an inspiration she is… a wonderful set up and a fantastic mix of facts and personal experiences."
Rachel Gray, Kindergarten Teacher & Mother

"The book is amazing and shows off a very talented writer… so proud of your thoughtfulness and carefully crafted writing… informative and inspiring as well.. I know you are having an impact and helping many of those in need."
Jennifer Kelly, Elementary School Teacher & Mother

This book is dedicated to those who aspire to make the world a better place. To this end, at least half of the proceeds from the sale of this book will be donated to Akhand Jyoti Eye Hospital (AJEH) in India. By buying this book you will be helping the blind, the poor, and the less privileged... while also reducing gender inequality and human trafficking!

1 out of 3 blind people in the world live in India!

AJEH performs more than 60,000 sight restoring surgeries per year!

It costs less than US$50 to restore someone's sight and change their life!!

AJEH's vision is to help eliminate curable blindness. They do this by providing affordable and high-quality eye care services to poor people in rural India. I was shocked to learn that the combination of blindness, poverty, and ignorance literally threatens the life of many girls my age!

AJEH seeks to improve the life of the girl child through unique initiatives like their "Football to Eyeball" program. The program offers girls education and career opportunities to eventually become optometrists – primary eye care specialists. This also leads to a broader impact in the local society, as the girls develop into role models and change agents. Stories on AJEH's website are sure to bring tears to anyone's eyes.
(www.akhandjyoti.org/)

In its first 14 years, AJEH has touched the lives of more than **12 million poor people**. Their work has not only restored vision but also the hopes and livelihoods of the poor. They do 80% of the sight-restoring surgeries for free! This is made possible through the constant support of well-wishers making donations.

Let us all please join AJEH in this crusade.

Table of Contents

8   Preface

10   Dr. Deepak Bhatia ~ Orthopedic Surgeon

14   Dr. Neha Kothari ~ Neuro-Physio Therapist

18   Dr. Pratik Kalani ~ Family Physician

22   Dr. Yashita Upadhyaya ~ General Surgeon

26   Vicky Ward ~ Dancer & Entrepreneur

30 Andrew Cowley ~ Aerialist & Dance Teacher

34 Tomas Biernacki ~ Director of Tennis & Coach

38 Jack Konieczny ~ Tennis Coach

42 Laura Terrile ~ School Teacher

46 Dr. Sarah Farris ~ School Counselor

50 Postface

Hi! I am **Bhavina Farswani**, the author of this book. I am an American of Indian descent and live with my family in Singapore. Curious and social by nature, I love reading, dancing, sports, traveling, and, most of all, spending time with my friends! I am currently a Grade 4 student at The Singapore American School.

Given the challenges posed by COVID19 in early 2020, we were forced to embrace distance learning. I missed the classroom environment, especially the fun interaction with my friends and teachers. With all the extra time and to focus my curious mind, my Mom arranged for me to have several conversations with some amazing people. She chose some surgeons, doctors, teachers, and coaches who have been active despite the difficulties presented during this pandemic. I will always be indebted to these everyday heroes for taking the time to talk to me.

I decided to publish this compilation of interviews so that others can also be inspired and we can raise money for a good cause. The general theme of my interviews covered questions like:

- *What motivates people to pursue professions that help humanity?*
- *What does it take to become a skilled professional?*

While the detailed interviews can be found on my website eventually, in this book I have tried to summarize information I learned during and after each interview. Beyond the specific answers to my prepared questions, I was surprised by the amount of new information that I learned. You will also find a few overall takeaways highlighted in the Postface section.

Hope you enjoy reading this book!

Dr. Deepak Bhatia

Orthopedic Specialist (Knee & Shoulder)
Al Zahra Hospital, United Arab Emirates

Schooling
The United Kingdom & United Arab Emirates

Higher Education
Bachelor of Medicine, Bachelor of Surgery (MBBS)
Fellowship of the Royal College of Surgeons (Edinburgh & Glasgow)
Fellowship at John Hopkins Hospital (U.S.A.)

Professional Description
Orthopedic surgeons are specialists in the musculoskeletal system. They address any disorders and injuries using a variety of medical tools, scans, and medical procedures before engaging in active surgery.

Professional Impact
Dr. Bhatia has successfully completed more than 20,000 surgeries and treated twice as many patients during his career thus far.

His Story

Unlike others, Dr. Bhatia was inspired to become an orthopedic surgeon at a party. Yep! You heard me right. At a party!

Born in Scotland to a physician, he was subsequently raised in London and Dubai. During his younger years, he was teased by his friends for being left-handed and this made him feel like he had a disability. However, one evening while helping serve food at a house party, he saw a famous orthopedic surgeon getting a lot of respect and it was obvious he was also left-handed. This changed the young man's perspective and inspired him to follow the footsteps of the famous surgeon.

Today, Dr. Bhatia is a consultant and surgeon at Al Zahra Hospital in Sharjah and Dubai. To get to where he is today, it took him 6 years to become a certified doctor and another 10 years to become a certified surgeon. He has been practicing surgery and gaining invaluable experience for almost 30 years! While Dr. Bhatia works long hours, seeing patients, and conducting 10 surgeries per week, work is "never tedious" to him because it's his passion. He recalls the time when he worked more than 100 hours per week in London as a junior surgeon and feels that one gets used to the hours "when you love what you do." COVID19 has increased the need for testing and protective equipment but has not affected his routine much.

One would think that someone like him would not have any time for hobbies; however, Dr. Bhatia makes time for things he enjoys: gardening, playing the drums, listening to music, and driving his sports car.

Other Lessons From my Conversation

Did you know?

- 40% of surgeons are left-handed but only 10% of the global population is left-handed

- Since bones are dense, orthopedic surgery requires many motorized tools

- Surgeons used to work more than 100 hours a week to gain experience & earn the title of consultant. Now it's limited to 50-60 hours a week.

Keyhole surgery

Orthopedic surgeons have found a way to repair the bone and cartilage by just making a small cut in the knee! The procedure uses long pencil-like instruments called arthroscopes. These can fit through the small cuts. They contain within them many parts, including a camera with a viewing device, lens cleaner, and an energy-supply device. The advantages for the patient are many – smaller scars, shorter hospital recovery, and less trauma. After the surgery, the patient does require special treatment from a trained physical therapist.

COVID19 impact

"As an orthopedic surgeon, my team and I get tested every week and if the results are negative we are okay to see patients. But, if the patient tests positive then they can't come to the clinic. Patients are only allowed to visit the clinic if their test results are negative, and even then for safety we wear full protective gear, including mask, gown, and gloves."

Dr. Neha Kothari

Neuro-Physio Therapist & Founder
Seventh Sense Movement Center, India

Schooling
Mumbai, India

Higher Education
Bachelor's Degree in Physical Therapy, KEM Medical College – India.

Professional Description
Neurological physical therapy helps treat and manage the symptoms of those dealing with nervous system damage to improve mobility and how a person functions in day-to-day life.

Professional Impact
Dr. Kothari has treated more than 20,000 patients during her career thus far.

Her story

Like the brilliant facets of the diamonds that her husband sells, Dr. Kothari's brilliance shows despite her simplicity! She was shy to talk about herself but quickly energized when I showed an interest in her field of study.

Born and raised in India, Dr. Kothari was an active and curious child. She indulged in aquatic sports, Bharatanatyam & Kathak dancing, music, camping, and "...everything outdoorsy". I was very curious about why she chose to be a physical therapist. Dr. Kothari explained that "...all the family dinners during her childhood were non-stop discussions about patients and their illnesses." She never liked that. She wanted everything in balance. Also, she preferred to help people using her hands and not with medicines. Eventually, she followed the footsteps of her charismatic aunt who is an accomplished physical therapist and holistic healer.

Today Dr. Kothari is a renowned Neuro-Physiotherapist. She also co-founded The Seventh Sense Movement Centre with her sister and brother. The center is a "...multi-disciplinary initiative" to help proactively improve the quality of life. Dr. Kothari's teacher, coach, and mentor was the renowned Dr. Nandu Chabbria at Sir HN Hospital in Mumbai. He trained her to go beyond treating symptoms and treat the root cause of the patient's problem. To this end, beyond the traditional decade of medical education and training, Dr. Kothari continues to expand her understanding of mind and body. She continues to study Neuroscience, Cranio-Sacral & Sound Therapy, Visceral Manipulation, Watsu & Aquatic Therapy, Pilates, and Yoga. Her sincerity and dedication to her profession have earned her a strong fan following in India and abroad.

Also a mother of two grown sons now, she continues to find time for music and the arts. She loves to play her sitar and has inspired her sons to play the santoor (a string instrument) and the tablas (a bass instrument). I believe her husband has a good ear for music too!

other Lessons From my Conversation

Advice For the young

- "...Don't stop exploring just because of competition or peer pressure..."

- "Don't eat too much junk food because that affects your body. By the time you are in your tweens, it makes it harder for you to enjoy many of your hobbies!"

- "Immunity is a feeling of inner strength. The body sends signals when there is an internal imbalance. We should not ignore these signals. Also, diet and sleep are critical to strong immunity."

Movement is Key to High Quality Life

In today's world, everyone is careful about their health. There is also sensory overload due to digital media. Neuro-Physio Therapy is a deeper study of brain function and its impact on physical movement. Her mentor, Dr. Chhabria, was a pioneer in this field and trained her to "...listen to the patient for the diagnosis."

In Dr. Kothari's practice, she blends lessons from her diverse experiences into tailored "movement routines". She combines ancient Yoga practices with modern science. Commonly referred to as "Kinetics," this approach has brought recovery and movement solutions to many who are suffering from ailments and pain. Kinetics emphasizes inter-disciplinary and inter-professional approaches to the understanding of physical activity and overall health. For example, emotional stress is often a root cause of problems in the modern world. So mind-trainers and occupational therapists are invited to run sessions too.

Fun Facts

- Our strongest muscle is... in the jaw!
- Our biggest muscle is... the gluteus maximus or the bottom!
- Our smallest muscle is... the stapes in the ear!
- We bend our fingers... 25 million times in a lifetime!
- Our brain is as small as... two fists put together!
- Our brain produces... 100,000 reactions per second!
- Our nose can smell... 3000 different smells!
- Our eyes can see... 10 million different hues!
- Our body produces sweat... to cool down!

Dr. Pratik Kalani

Family Physician
Niagara Health System, Canada

Schooling
The United Arab Emirates and Canada

Higher Education
Bachelor of Health Sciences at McMaster University, Ontario – Canada
Doctor of Medicine (MD) at McMaster University, Ontario – Canada
Family Medicine Residency Training Program at Western University, Ontario - Canada

Professional Description
Family physicians help patients of all ages and are at the frontline of the medical community. They are experts at managing common complaints, recognizing important diseases, uncovering hidden conditions, and managing most acute and chronic illnesses. They emphasize health promotion and disease prevention.

Professional Impact
Dr. Kalani has treated more than 20,000 patients so far. Since the COVID19 pandemic began, Dr. Kalani has tested over 5,000 patients.

His Story

Born in India, Dr. Kalani went to school in Dubai before his family migrated to Canada. I think all parents believe it is their job to feed the curious minds and growing bodies of their children. So it would seem Dr. Kalani's parents did a good job! Today, both their sons - Dr. Pratik Kalani & Dr. Aashish Kalani are thriving medical experts in Canada.

As a child, Dr. Pratik Kalani was always interested in science and math. Besides doing well in class, he enthusiastically competed in annual elementary school trivia contests called Math Olympiads. After moving to Canada in Grade 4, his interest in Science quickly grew, and soon "...his heart was set on fixing people with his brain."

I asked Dr. Kalani why he chose family medicine and was delighted to hear that interviewing people had something to do with it! During university, Dr. Kalani hosted a weekly campus radio program called "Health Justice Radio". This gave him the opportunity to talk to important members of the community, and understand the challenges of providing care to the underserved. This experience convinced him that only a family doctor can be a part of a patient's full journey. Dr. Kalani is delighted that he is the first one that patients see when they have a problem. Many of his patients consider him part of their family. Some patients bring him homemade baked goodies during the holiday season, and some stop by to check on his health!

Family physicians can have a fairly balanced life in Canada. During his free time, Dr. Kalani makes time for his parents and family, as well as fun hobbies like watching F1 car racing or playing video games. His wife is my next interviewee!

other Lessons From my Conversation

- On average, family physicians see more than 80 patients a week!

- According to research done in the United States of America, adding one family doctor for every 10,000 people can lower emergency room visits by 11%!

- Approximate half of all medical visits are made to primary care physicians like family doctors, yet the number of medical students choosing this field is declining! According to Dr. Kalani, this may be because people don't put enough value on preventative care, but are willing to pay much more for medical care after they have fallen seriously ill.

Advice For the Young

Dr. Kalani believes very strongly that "...practicing medicine is both an art and a science, so make sure to place your interests in both of these fields!" Being an effective medical professional is as much about the knowledge of sciences as it is about the art of applying that knowledge, and understanding human society.

Facts about the Human Body

The human body is made of approximately 206 bones which are connected by about 100 joints, forming the skeletal system. This structure is then covered by muscles, ligaments, and fat tissue, giving the human body its natural form. Muscles are made from fiber that look like a piece of thin string and make our bones, eyes, our heart, and other body parts move. This forms the muscular system. Sweeping across the first two systems is the nervous system. Nerves carry teeny tiny neurons that enable the brain to tell the muscle of its choice what to do and when. In fact, the brain is the organ that has control over our full body, including the respiratory, circulatory & digestive systems. These other systems basically provided the full body with critical oxygen, blood, and nutrition, while allowing excretion of that which is not good for the body.

Dr. Yashita Upadhyaya

Pharmacist & General Surgeon
Niagara Health System, Canada

Schooling
Canada

Higher Education
Doctor of Pharmacy (Pharm.D.) at University of Toledo, Ohio - USA
Doctor of Medicine (M.D., C.M.) at McGill University, Montreal – Canada
Post-Graduate General Surgery Residency Training Program at McMaster University, Ontario - Canada

Professional Description
A pharmacist helps visitors at pharmacies choose the right medicine and how to take them safely.
A general surgeon focuses on performing surgery in the abdomen area.

Professional Impact
During her brief career as a pharmacist, Dr. Yashita filled over 20,000 prescriptions and administered more than 200 flu shots. As a trainee surgeon, she has performed and assisted with over 1,000 surgeries.

Her Story

Born in the pride lands of Africa, Dr. Yashita has an interesting story that traverses two continents and three professional pursuits! She is a "... hands-on person who loves to be in the operating room..." and thinks treating patients is a privilege. I loved hearing her compare dancing to surgery!

Neuro-surgery was her preference in Grade 10, but she changed her mind and chose to study pharmacy eventually. She liked the idea of being able to help patients in all situations. However, after working as a pharmacist for a year, she did not find her work satisfying. Hence, Dr. Yashita decided to go back to university and study surgery!

Given all the hard work she has had to do, I thought she would not have time for hobbies. Just not true! Dr. Yashita still finds the time for Bharatanatyam dancing, playing soccer, and field hockey! In fact, she believes all her training in dance has equipped her for a career in surgery. She explains, "...Both are sequential. I am not just executing precise movements from memory, but I am also planning and reacting to the world around me. Through dance, I use well-articulated movements and expressions to draw my audience in as I perform a story. In surgery, through my training, I draw on my understanding of the various sciences and technical skills to perform an operation. I find this exhilarating. It is why I will continue to dance and it is why I pursue surgery with such vigor!"

Dr. Yashita is as energetic in person as she sounds. She is also very dedicated. Throughout the COVID19 pandemic, she has not missed a single day of university or hospital. To stay safe, she has been wearing protective gear.

Other Lessons From my Conversation

- Since 2000, all pharmacists need to hold a doctorate degree!

- More than 90% of people live within 5 miles of a pharmacist!

- There are more than 20 types of surgeons... general surgeons require a broad knowledge of the body and surgical procedures, whereas other surgeons are more specialized.

- Almost half of all medical school graduates are now women!

- Only about 19 percent of all surgeons today are women but that number is growing!

- Research has shown that female doctors are more likely to follow medical guidelines, collaborate with their workmates, communicate better with their patients, and adopt a patient-centered approach to care!

Indian Classical Dance

There are eight traditional Indian dances, these include Bharatanatyam, Kathak, Kuchipudi, Odissi, Manipuri, Sattriya, Mohiniyattam, and the Bhangra.

While the Bhangra has worldwide popularity, Bharatanatyam is the most ancient of all the Indian Classical Dance forms.

Bharatnatyam style is noted for its fixed upper torso, bent legs, and knees flexed combined with spectacular footwork. It contains at least 20 Asanas (poses) found in modern yoga.

Advice For the Young

Dr. Yashita was quick to highlight that "...it is important to do well but remember that it's a long road. Don't worry if you want to take a break in between the undergraduate years to explore other options!" Getting to know ourselves is critical to having a future plan that we can be happy with.

Vicky Lee Ward

Dancer and Founder,
All That Jazz Dance Academy, Singapore

Schooling
Canada

Higher Education
Master of Arts in Professional Practice (Arts Management), Middlesex University, U.K.
Higher National Diploma in Professional Dance and Musical Theatre, Trinity College, U.K.
Performer's Diploma, Urdang Academy of Performing Arts, U.K.
Associate Ballet, Imperial Society Teachers of Dancing (ISTD), U.K.
ADAPT Jazz, Tap & Ballet Certified Teacher, Associate Dance Arts for Professional Teachers (ADAPT), Canada

Professional Description
Dance teachers provide students with a high standard of artistic dance education to inspire and foster excellence in the arts. Ms. Vicky's aim is to preserve and promote the art of dance through performance, education, and outreach. She places emphasis on classical ballet training as a foundation for all dance classes at her academy.

Professional Impact
During her career thus far, Ms. Vicky has taught dance to more than 20,000 students in Canada, the United Kingdom, the United States of America, and now Singapore!

Her Story

Ms. Vicky runs the dance school where my little sister Urvina and I have been learning Ballet, Jazz & Tap for several years – The All That Jazz Dance Academy. I am totally in awe of her! Teacher, Performance Team Coach, Business Owner, and Mother. She does it all!

Ms. Vicky was born in Malaysia but migrated to Canada when she was about 10 years old. While in Malaysia, she was fortunate to get trained by Ms. Lee Lee Lan – the first Asian to be appointed examiner by the Imperial Society of Teachers of Dancing (ISTD) for ballet, modern dance, and tap! Ms. Vicky's early passion for dance and that strong foundational training won her many opportunities to dance competitively and also at national arts events. I was amazed to hear that she even performed for advertisements of Looney Tunes, Coke, and other brands. She was less than 10 years old, and got paid "$200-300 per gig"... unbelievable!

After graduating from high school in Vancouver, I was curious why she enrolled at a dance school in London. She explained that Urdang Academy is one of the best places to study degree level musical theatre and professional dance. Since students spend 10 hours a day in the dance studio she never felt alone. Just very tired! Ms. Vicky's passion and hard work did not go unnoticed. After her first year of training at Urdang Academy, she was granted a full scholarship by Ms. Leonie Urdang who founded the academy!

While pursuing her diploma at the Urdang Academy, Ms. Vicky also completed her teaching certification from the ISTD in London! Soon after, she was on the move again! She danced intensively with well-known teachers and choreographers at Broadway Dance Center in New York and also The Edge Performing Arts Studio in Los Angeles. The experiences taught her to stay humble, celebrate wins, and graciously accept losses. After four years in the USA, she followed the footsteps of her first teacher and moved to Asia to open her own studio.

My sister and friends love our time at Ms. Vicky's dance school because her motto is to balance fun with discipline. She wants us to be inspired to be strong dancers who value teamwork, persistence, and humility. I have personally experienced this when we perform together as a team at competitions and shows. Ms. Vicky and the other teachers are beautiful, graceful, fun-loving, and very dedicated to music and dance. Baking and family are the only things that can get in the way!

Other Lessons From My Conversation

- Ballet originated in Italy, not France or Russia!

- The very first ballet dancers were men! This was because women were not allowed to dance in public until 1681, and therefore unable to join the ballet.

- To perform in a ballet, the amount of energy required is roughly the same as playing 2 full football matches, or running 28.9 km!

- Gymnasts are recognized as athletes but dancers are not!

- There are 5 levels of graduation in a ballet company... A dancer would start as (1) Apprentice, then become a (2) Corps de Ballet, before getting promoted to (3) Demi-soloist (second soloist), and subsequently (4) Soloist (first soloist). Exceptionally good dancers, eventually get the rank of (5) Principal Dancer.

COVID19 impact on the Profession

Due to COVID19, all dance studios in Singapore had to be closed down suddenly. Ms. Vicky quickly developed an online teaching strategy to continue to provide students a full dance class experience at home. She helped all the teachers modify their lesson plans, while her tech-savvy husband helped her set-up the portal. All the students would be dancing at home! It turned out to be lots of fun! Ms. Vicky even got an Entrepreneurship Award for her resourcefulness during a tough period for everyone.

Advice For Young People

''...uncertainty, challenges, and emotional upheavals are all part of life and we must always look forward... follow our heart and family... enjoy life, pizza, and ice cream. Never give in to peer pressure... stay true to yourself!''

Andrew Cowley

Aerialist & Dance Teacher
All That Jazz Dance Academy, Singapore

Schooling
United Kingdom

Higher Education
Diploma in Dance, Performance Academy (U.K.)

Professional Description
A dance teacher teaches technique, performance, and choreography. A good dance teacher also provides strength training because dancers must be strong and flexible. They help students prepare mentally and physically for competitions, exams, and everything in between!

Professional Impact
Coach Andi has performed for more than 2 million people and trained more than 2,000 students during his career thus far.

His Story

At first glance, Coach Andi is a fun and goofy teacher who is very high energy. However, once I saw him perform Hip-hop, Jazz, Tap & Acro routines, I was impressed. He is a true artist who experiments with different dance styles, and even performed as an aerial artist!

Coach Andi's dream as a child was always to be a dancer. He started dance classes at the age of 6 at the Julie Bromage Dance Academy. During that time, he recalls training in the studio 6 days a week! His teachers were very strict about focus and posture, and students were not even allowed to sit down on the floor or lean against the wall during class. Thanks to this disciplined foundation, young Andi performed in famous venues like Royal Albert Hall and Sadler's Wells in London, and also Paris Disneyland! After getting his teaching qualification from the Imperial Society of Teachers of Dancing (ISTD), he accepted the opportunity to travel the world and perform for international audiences for 7 years on Royal Caribbean International's cruise liners! Seeing his strong talent, Coach Andi was given the opportunity to become an aerial artist on the cruise and eventually even lead the aerial team on the ship.

Coach Andi believes that a dancer is not just an artist but an athlete too. He says "...scientific studies show that the human body wasn't made for dance but humans have been mastering control of their body in their own personal ways... so dance gives humans a way to express themselves and allows music to be a 3D experience!" Given the physical strength required, he encourages us to eat healthy and nutritious foods with natural sugar (fruits) and nuts (slow-burning energy).

Since teaching is exhausting, he enjoys playing video games, cooking, and reading. He is getting married soon so I reckon that wedding planning is his new hobby!

Other Lessons From My Conversation

● There are more than 300 cruise ships in the world, and more than a thousand artists are onboard entertaining passengers. Coach Andi performed for the Royal Caribbean Cruise Lines!

● Depending on the cruise, artists perform a variety of roles in different shows so that guests onboard don't get bored. Since there is a limit on how many staff they can hire, each artist has to be very versatile.

● An aerial artist is usually the star feature of famous circus acts like Cirque de Soleil. I think of it as a combination of gymnastics and dance but at dangerous heights. The performer must have a strong core to be able to balance and control their movements while holding on to solid shapes that are suspended in air or even two very strong elastic ribbons. In case of a fall, each performer wears safety belts around their waist since there are no safety nets below to catch them. These safety belts are well hidden under their costumes.

● Dancers usually wear specially designed clothes called "leotards". "Leotard" is named after Jules Léotard. He was a French acrobatic performer and aerialist. He was also the one who developed the art of trapeze!

Advice For a Good Life

"... from a teacher standpoint, remember why you love to dance... life presents a lot of trials and tribulations and we always have to remind ourselves why we have chosen a certain path or project. To sustain the chosen path we have to be clear on the purpose or motivation."

Tomas Biernacki

Director of Tennis & Coach
Singapore American Club, Singapore

Schooling
Sweden

Higher Education
Various tennis certifications

Professional Description
A tennis coach is one who teaches students how to play tennis, improve their understanding of tennis, and the skills that are necessary to play well. As the director of the tennis program, Coach Tomas also has to develop training programs. He also coordinates the roster of all the coaches and students.

Professional Impact
Coach Tomas has trained thousands of students during his career thus far, including more than 20 students who pursued professional tennis. When he was the National Coach for Denmark & Sweden, he also coached 12 players who were among the top players in the world!

His story

Coach Tomas Beirnaki was born and raised in Sweden and has been playing tennis all his life. After working with several successful clubs in Sweden, he was selected to help the Swedish National Team and later became the National Coach for Denmark!

Throughout his childhood, Coach Tomas's dream was always to be a tennis player who competed in international Grand Slam Tournaments. However, an unfortunate injury prevented him from pursuing his dream. Instead of feeling bad for himself, I was amazed to learn that Coach Tomas quickly focused his passion for tennis on coaching. Since this was his weekend job since he was 14 years old, he knew he was good at this. After several years of coaching at national clubs where they successfully groomed several champions, he was chosen to coach and travel with the Swedish National Team. His success and dedication then won him the role of National Coach for Denmark. The teams he coached competed in prestigious tournaments like the Davis Cup, Fed Cup, and Grand Slams!

As the illustration shows, I am always surprised by how he stays so calm all day on a court full of young kids under the blazing Singapore sun. When I asked him his secret, Coach Tomas explained that "as a child, he threw "amazing" tantrums himself...," and his professional training has helped him better understand human behavior. When he sees a student get angry or frustrated, he gets down to their eye level so that he can engage in a calm conversation that would help the child find perspective. He walks them through what happened, why it happened, and what we can do about this. Coach Tomas believes that it is the job of the coach to keep motivating the student. However, "...it is a 50-50 kind of deal..." so the child gives 50% and the coach gives 50% to make a hundred percent required for success. It takes some of us time to adjust but eventually we all have to step-up if we enjoy it!

Besides tennis, Coach Tomas also enjoys traveling, reading, racing sports, and hitting the gym for a hard workout. He is proficient in English, Swedish, Polish, and German, with a basic command of Serbian and Croatian. So talented!

Other Lessons From my Conversation

Did you know?

In tennis, there are four annual international competitions which are very important. The term Grand Slam refers to winning all four of these major international tennis championships in the same calendar year:

- The Australian Open (played in January on hard courts)
- The Wimbledon in the United Kingdom (played in July/July on grass courts)
- The French Open (played in May/June on red clay courts)
- The US Open (played in August/September on hard courts)

Unlike many other sports, tennis coaches are not allowed to "coach" a player during a match in any of the Grand Slam tournaments!

Advice For young People

There are 10 behaviors that require little talent, but can create a big advantage for those who make these a habit:

Be on **TIME**

Be **Energy** high

Have a **Positive attitude**

Make an **EFFORT**

Do a little **extra**

Be **Coachable**

Have a strong **work ethic**

Be **Prepared**

Use good **body language**

Be **Passionate**

Jack Konieczny

Tennis Coach
Singapore American Club, Singapore

Schooling
Poland

Higher Education
Absolutorium in Economics & Marketing, University of Gdansk, Poland.
Certifications from Professional Tennis Registry
Polish Tennis Association Coaching License

Professional Description
A tennis coach is one who teaches students how to play tennis, improve their understanding of tennis, and the skills that are necessary to play well.

Professional Impact
Coach Jack has trained thousands of students during his career thus far!

His Story

Coach Jack has been playing tennis since he was 6 years old, and his father was a coach too! He is awesome on the court and has been training our entire family for the past year!

Coach Jack was born in Poland and grew up in a very sporty family. His Dad was a sports coach and businessman, and this inspired the love for sports in the children. Soon after he picked up the tennis racquet for the first time, Coach Jack was competing in tennis tournaments. By the time he was a teenager, he was competing in the Polish National Tennis Circuit organized by the Polish Tennis Association. However, this did not continue for long. It made me sad to hear that training to become a professional tennis player is very expensive.

When Coach Jack was about 14 years old, there was a global economic crisis, and his family was affected financially. So instead of paying money for coaching and working on improving his own game, Coach Jack started working part-time as a tennis buddy and tennis coach! For him the choice was easy. He loved his family and wanted to be of help.

Upon graduating from high school, he decided to follow in his father's footsteps by getting a degree in Economics and Marketing. Like a true sportsman, he focused on the game that was in front of him. He did not waste time and energy in feeling bad for himself. Instead, he started a coffee shop business to support himself! After graduation, he returned to teaching tennis full time. He started coaching in Poland before moving to Singapore.

Other than tennis, he loves windsurfing, alpine skiing, and watching others play volleyball. At 5 feet 9 inches, he thinks he is too short to play! Hilarious right?!

Other Lessons From My Conversation

Did you know?

- There are 1,814 male and 1,106 female professional tennis players who are ranked!

- The British Lawn Tennis Association estimates it costs almost US$400,000 to develop a player from age 5 to 18.

- The U.S. Tennis Association estimates that the annual average cost to be a "highly competitive" professional tennis player is more than US$140,000. This includes US$70,000 for coaching and US$60,000 for travel!

- Tennis professionals earn money by advertising for companies, showing up at events, and doing well at tennis tournaments. According to information on the internet, the following is the prize money at Grand Slam tournaments. Typically the champion's coach would get 10% of the prize money:

	Champion's Prize Money
2019 U.S. Open	$3,850,000
2019 Australian Open	$2,780,000
2019 French Open	$2,524,000
2019 Wimbledon	$3,486,000

- In 2019, the International Tennis Federation published its first global report. According to the report, there are almost 90 million tennis players in more than 195 countries. China, the USA, India, Germany, and the United Kingdom are the top 5 tennis-playing countries.

Advice For Young People

- "..always enjoy what you are doing!"

- "Treat your heroes as an example. Never feel overwhelmed with other's achievements. You should admire other's accomplishments, get inspired, and aim for your own dreams at the same time!"

Laura Terrile

Teacher
Singapore American School, Singapore

Schooling
New York

Higher Education
Bachelor of Science, Syracuse University, New York
Master of Science, The College of St. Rose, New York

Professional Description
Teachers are the most important part of our society. They give children a purpose and set them up for life with broad skills and knowledge. They provide a strong foundational base for the citizens and leaders of the future.

Professional Impact
During the course of her 25-year career, Mrs. Terrile has taught more than 500 students in elementary school.

Her story

I am blessed with the best and most awesome teachers each year. There was Ms. Sarah, Ms. Marisol, Ms. Peggy, Ms. Gray, Ms. Kelly, Ms. DeMichael, and then Mrs. Bolton and Mrs. Terrile in Grade 3. Since I observed Mrs. Terrile manage through COVID19 challenges cool as a cucumber, I spoke to her about her life and how she manages stress.

Growing up in the United States of America, Mrs. Terrile looked forward to international experiences and jumped at the opportunity to teach us at the Singapore American School. To become an elementary school teacher, she earned her degrees in teaching in rapid succession. I was surprised to know that, similar to the medical professionals, teachers also have to get extensive practical experience. To groom her skills, Mrs. Terrile taught in two different grade levels.

Since my parents are always telling me how their school experience was so different, I asked Mrs. Terrile how a teacher's job has changed in 20 years. She explained that "...the methods of training, lesson content, behavioral science, and crowd management have all evolved with the progression of technology and society." Since our school has such a diverse student community, I was pleased to learn that "at the start of every academic year, community building and student assessments are given importance. Focus is on creating a calm and safe learning environment for the unique children in the class." Based on this initial phase, our teachers find creative strategies to accelerate our personal learning. For example, since I love to dance then she might ask me to write about dance so that writing becomes fun for me!

After a full day of managing 23 students, Mrs. Terrile returns home to two amazing children of her own. Hence she has to be mindful, calm, and peaceful so that she can give her best to everyone. I have no idea how she does that so well!

Other Lessons From my Conversation

Did you know?

- My school is almost 65 years old! Singapore American School (SAS) was established by the American Association of Malaya in January 1956. It was originally intended as a school for the children of American executives, missionaries, and diplomats who did not want to follow the British practice of sending school-aged children home to boarding schools. SAS is one of the best international schools in the world because of the learning system, caring teachers, and supportive staff.

- There are two methods of elementary teaching: The Reggio Emilia and Montessori systems. These early-childhood educational methods are similar in some ways but have alternative approaches to nurturing each child. Basically, the Reggio Emilia system is focused on group learning and discovery, while the Montessori system allows children to work and learn at their own pace. At SAS, our teachers mix the approaches so we get the best of both. While the Reggio Emilia approach is used for writing, math, reading, and testing, time is also set aside for individual development every week.

COVID19 impact on the Profession

In response to the country-wide lockdown, SAS moved all the students and teachers to a distance-learning format. The early days were tough for the teachers and students because of the distance, and technical glitches. But thanks to the support from the SAS management team, teachers found ways to overcome the obstacles. Soon the teachers were thinking of creative ways to improve their methods of training so that we achieved learning objectives with minimum screen time!

Dr. Sarah Farris

Elementary School Counselor
Singapore American School, Singapore

Schooling
The United States of America

Higher Education
Bachelor of Arts, George Mason University
Master of Arts in Education, University of Central Florida
Master of Education in Counseling, Lehigh University
Doctor in Educational Leadership, University of Southern California

Professional Description
There are two types of counselors: School Counselor and Guidance Counselor. A school counselor helps with mindfulness, socio-emotional learning, and school-related problems and how to solve them. On the other hand, a guidance counselor helps high school students choose a college or university.

Professional Impact
During her professional career, Dr. Farris has counseled more than 2,000 children and students.

Her story

Dr. Farris has been my school counselor since I joined Singapore American School's Early Learning Center. She is full of strategies to deal with all the possible challenges we face as children. Talking to her was very interesting, as always!

As a child, Dr. Farris was interested in a lot of things. Curious by nature, she kept learning, growing, and keeping an open mind... I have heard people say "Curiosity kills the Cat", but in her case, it took her to Africa! After high school, Dr. Farris joined the United States Peace Corps and moved to Africa to work in elementary schools. This experience helped her decide that she would pursue a Bachelor's and Master's Degree in education! Right after graduation, she found her wings again and this time moved to Singapore to teach at my school – the Singapore American School (SAS)!

After a few years of teaching elementary school students, Dr. Farris was fascinated by the role of the student counselor. She felt it would allow her to build closer relationships with a larger group of children. So she dedicated her evenings to studying for a second Master's Degree followed by a Doctorate Degree, this time in counseling and leadership. She says, "...I believe that it is important to be happy in everything that you do."

After 2 years of studying and 100 hours of practical training, Dr. Farris finally earned the title of Doctor and SAS was glad to offer her a role as Elementary School Counselor. As a counselor, she is regularly teaching us how to be awesome human beings by developing "critical people skills". She says that "...life can be hard if you don't know how to work with people and your emotions."

I love Dr. Farris because she is a good listener, very patient and most importantly has a big heart!

Other Lessons From My Conversation

Did You Know?

The United States Peace Corps (pronounced "Peace Core"), is an organization that is trying to put an end to world hunger and many other social development challenges. The Peace Corps is a volunteer organization that provides service opportunities to those who want to bring change by working closely with local communities all around the world on pressing challenges, including education.

Advice For Young People

- "Children should be safe, responsible, and kind. Also, it is important to learn how to laugh and have a growth mindset at all times." Growth mindset requires a person to believe in themselves and have the confidence that by trying difficult things we can grow our intellect and abilities. It is about having a positive mindset and letting go of negative thoughts. Think before you feel and do!

- Dr. Farris comes to class regularly to explain to us the importance of being respectful, honest, fair, responsible, and compassionate at all times. While our school teachers give us a strong academic foundation, she helps us build skills in the social-emotional realm. "Social-emotional learning (SEL) is the process of developing the self-awareness, self-control, and interpersonal skills that are vital for success at school, work, and life."

POSTFACE

It has been 4 months since I embarked on what sounded like fun chit-chats with people I know. In the process, I have learned a few things that will stay with me forever:

- Most successful people have at least one hobby like music, dance or sports!

- All good work has its own set of challenges… A diamond sparkles only after the stone is appropriately polished!

- There is more to a person than their current profession or occupation. We should not judge a book by its cover!

- Success depends on how we deal with problems not by avoiding them. Nothing ventured, nothing gained at all!

- For best results, we should use good listening skills, get a holistic understanding of the problem, and then use critical thinking to find a solution. Let's not look at the world through a keyhole!